MVP
SPORTS
PUZZLES

BY BRAD HERZOG
AND THE EDITORS OF
SPORTS ILLUSTRATED FOR KIDS

A *Sports Illustrated For Kids* Book

BANTAM BOOKS
TORONTO • NEW YORK • LONDON • SYDNEY • AUCKLAND

MVP Sports Puzzles by Brad Herzog

A Bantam Book/February 1995

Sports Illustrated For Kids and **KIDS** are registered trademarks of Time Inc. Sports Illustrated For Kids Books are published in cooperation with Bantam Doubleday Dell Publishing Group, Inc. under license from Time Inc.

Cover and interior design by Miriam Dustin
Cover illustration by Glenn Gustafson
Interior illustrations by Bob Staake

For information address: Bantam Books

ISBN 0-553-48288-2

Published simultaneously in the United States and Canada

Bantam books are published by Bantam Books, a division of Bantam Doubleday Dell Publishing Group, Inc. Its trademark, consisting of the words "Bantam Books" and the portrayal of a rooster, is Registered in the U.S. Patent and Trademark Office and in other countries. Marca Registrada. Bantam Books, 1540 Broadway, New York, NY 10036.

Printed in the United States of America

CWO 10 9 8 7 6 5 4 3 2 1

ARE YOU AN MVP?

In this league, MVP stands for Most Valuable *Puzzlemeister*. That's because the games you'll play are crosswords, word finds, jumbles, fill-ins, and other fun puzzles that all have one thing in common: To solve them, you have to know sports.

But wait! There's more. MVP *Sports Puzzles* will test your sports smarts further with *What's the Call?* brain teasers from the pages of *Sports Illustrated For Kids* magazine. In these puzzlers, you are the official, umpire, or referee. You are plunked down in the middle of a sporting event, and given a tough question about the rules. You must make the right call.

There's a lot of challenges inside, but you're made of championship stuff. So, go ahead. Give it your best shot, and see if you're an MVP!

SHAQ PACK

What athlete is big enough to hold the names of 17 other sports stars? Shaquille O'Neal, of course. Can you place the 17 current and former athletes listed on the next page in the proper spaces in the SHAQ word grid by using the number of letters in their last names? Four names have been put in place to give you a head start.

After you've filled in the rest, write the letters from the shaded boxes in the spaces below. Unscramble them to find the name of the university where Shaq was one terrific Tiger.

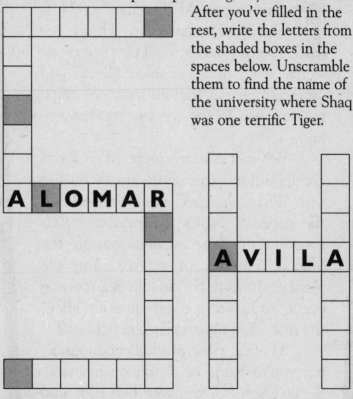

SCRAMBLED:

__ __ __ __ __ __ __ __ __ __ __

BASEBALL
Joe DIMAGGIO
Ted WILLIAMS
~~Bobby AVILA~~
Ryne SANDBERG
~~Eric DAVIS~~
Rick REUSCHEL
~~Roberto ALOMAR~~
Rod CAREW

TENNIS
~~Arthur ASHE~~
Mats WILANDER

FOOTBALL
Joe MONTANA
Dan MARINO
Bart STARR
Earl CAMPBELL

TRACK AND FIELD
Carl LEWIS

HOCKEY
Maurice RICHARD
Denis SAVARD

D A V I S

A
S
H
E

UNSCRAMBLED:

__ __ __ __ __ __ __ __

__ __ __ __

OUCH!

Matt "Splits" Fisher is an ace pitcher for the Kings. He is famous for his split-finger knuckleball, which is almost impossible to hit.

The Kings are playing the Orioles. The Kings lead 3-0 in the bottom of the seventh. Matt has been striking out batter after batter.

But Matt's arm is getting tired. He gives up two singles and a walk. The bases are loaded with two outs. Steve "Bubba" Parsons is at the plate for the Orioles.

The count is one ball and two strikes. Matt throws another split-finger pitch. The ball wiggles through the air. Steve swings and misses. At the last instant, the ball drops and hits Steve on the foot.

You're the umpire. What call do you make? Is that strike three, or does Steve head to first base because he was hit by the pitch?

WHAT'S IN A NAME?

The 10 words in the box below are used in a few different sports. They are also part of the names of some well-known athletes. Can you fit the sports words into the proper spaces to form the names of the sports stars? The first one is done for you.

> PUCK   ICE   RACE   BAT   NET
> MITT   ~~HIT~~   PAR   WALK   RANK

1. MARK W **H** **I** **T** EN

2. GABRIELA SA _B_ _a_ _t_ INI

3. DAVID JUST _i_ _c_ _e_

4. ROBERT _P_ _a_ _r_ ISH

5. F _R_ _a_ _n_ _k_ THOMAS

6. EM _m_ _i_ _t_ _t_ SMITH

7. KIRBY _P_ _u_ _c_ _k_ ETT

8. HO _r_ _a_ _c_ _e_ GRANT

9. LARRY _W_ _a_ _l_ _k_ ER

10. JA _n_ _e_ _t_ EVANS

OH SAY, CAN YOU "C"?

You'll soon "C" what letter is the star of this crossword puzzle. Use the following clues to fill in the crossword on the next page. All of the answers will begin with the letter "C."

ACROSS

1. The hometown of the Bears, Bulls, and Blackhawks
4. Texas Ranger slugger Will _____
5. Cleveland's NBA team
6. A teammate of the answer to 4 Across: Jose _____
8. This state is home to the Rams, Raiders, Chargers, and 49ers.
9. The person in charge of preparing a football team
11. The sound a bat makes when hitting a baseball
13. The fourth batter in a lineup is called the _____-up hitter.
14. Soccer's biggest event: the World _____
15. Boston Red Sox pitcher "Rocket" Roger _____
16. Teams from the University of Kentucky and Villanova University are nicknamed the Wild_____.

DOWN

1. The one fielder in baseball who faces the other fielders
2. The country that is home to the Vancouver Canucks
3. The area patrolled by a hockey goaltender
4. A competitor in the Indy 500 drives a race_____.
7. Joe _____ hit the home run that won the 1993 World Series for the Toronto Blue Jays.

1 Chicago **2** **3**

4 c
a

5 Cavaliers

6 **7**

8 California

9 **10**

11 crack **12**

13

14

15

16

8. Detroit Tiger first baseman _____ Fielder

10. Patrick Ewing's position

11. This team plays at Wrigley Field.

12. What tennis and basketball players play on

PASSING FANCY

The Pilgrims are playing the Turkeys in a Thanksgiving Day football classic. The Turkeys are getting their feathers plucked, 35-0. They have the ball and would be thankful to score just one touchdown. The ball is on the 50-yard line, it's fourth-and-20, and there's less than a minute to go in the game.

The Turkeys line up in their wishbone formation. Quarterback Gabby Gable takes the snap. He rolls right, looking to pass. After a few steps, he is hit by a Pilgrims' defensive end. As Gabby is falling, he spots a receiver just across the line of scrimmage. Gabby throws the ball underhand. The receiver grabs it and takes off. He runs 10 yards, 30 yards, 50 yards . . . *touchdown!* Now the Pilgrims are hopping mad. They complain that Gabby's pass was illegal. Was it?

STATES, MAN!

Each of the rhymes below describes a U.S. state. Print the state's name in the spaces below each rhyme. Copy the shaded letters into the spaces at the bottom of the page. Unscramble those letters to find the last name of a legendary athlete — and the name of another state!

1. This state cheers for the Rockets' Hakeem,
and Emmitt and Troy on America's Team.

T e X a S

2. In this southwestern state, it's not often raining.
That's why it's home to the Suns and spring training.

___ ___ ___ ___ ___ ___ ▓▓▓

3. The St. Louis Cardinals all dress in red,
but this state's hockey team is the Blues instead.

▓▓▓ ___ ___ ___ ___ ___ ___

4. Louisville Slugger bats come from this place.
It's also home to the Derby, a famous horse race.

___ ___ ▓▓▓ ___ ___ ___ ___ ___

5. This place is known as the Empire State.
Fans there think the Yankees and Bills are great.

▓▓▓ ___ ___ ___ ▓▓▓ ___ ___

SCRAMBLED: ___ ___ ___ ___ ___ ___ ___

UNSCRAMBLED: ___ ___ ___ ___ ___ ___ ___

11

INITIALS SEARCH

The word-grid on the following page is in the shape of the initials DH, which stands for designated hitter. Many words and phrases that are used in sports are often known by their initials. Look at the 17 sports words and phrases on this page, and write their proper initials in the space next to each one. Then go to the DH word-grid and find the initials there. They are written across and up and down. The first one is done for you.

1. base on balls **BB**

2. touchdown _____

3. stolen base _____

4. wide receiver WR

5. technical knockout _____

6. at-bats _____

7. field goal _____

8. power play goal (or points per game) _____

9. quarterback QB

10. sacrifice fly _____

11. point after touchdown _____

```
T K O P S        P C            L E
Z V R K H P      L D           (Q B)
L N A D J P V   (W R)           P O
I S       G B G  R A            K A
T F       R T    O V R B I H B
N E       E O    A M Y H T W F
O R       K D    Z I L E D X U
(B B)       N H G  P Y            L R
U X N P S H I    A H            F A
S J F L Y L      T Q            G V
B C N F L        F L            H R
```

12. National Hockey League NHL

13. home run _____

14. run batted in _____

15. National Football League NFL

16. timeout (or turnover) _____

17. putout _____

13

A REAL FOUL SHOT

Slye Foxx grew up playing basketball with her older brothers. They taught her how to shoot, pass, and dribble. They also taught her a few tricks.

In a youth-league game against the Bulldogs, Slye decides to try one of her tricks. She has just been fouled while scoring a lay-up, and she is ready to shoot one foul shot.

Slye thinks she knows a way to get *two* chances to make that shot. Standing at the free-throw line, she bounces the ball once, and then looks at the basket. She starts to shoot, but instead of releasing the ball, she holds on to it. A Bulldog player is faked out and steps into the free-throw lane for the rebound. But there's no shot! As soon as Slye sees the player in the lane, she does take her shot, but she misses.

Slye yells that she deserves another try. She says — correctly — that a free-throw shooter should get another attempt if an opposing player steps into the lane before the free throw hits the rim.

You are the referee. Does Slye get another shot?

DOUBLE PLAY

You'll earn a bonus when you solve this puzzle. Below are six great athletes' names with the letters all mixed up. Unscramble the names and write them in the spaces on the right. (HINT: The symbol is their sport.) Then write the letters from the shaded boxes in order in the Secret Name spaces to spell the name of another sports legend.

1. NEWRAR OMON ▢▢ __ __ __ __
   __ __ __ __ __

2. TWIL RCHLIMABEAN __ __ ▢▢
   __ __ __ __ __ __ __ __ __

3. SHIRC VTREE __ __ __ __ __
   ▢▢

4. LUPA TOILMOR ▢▢ __ __
   __ __ __ __ __ __ __

5. J. A. OFTY __. __. __ __ __ ▢▢

6. INBONE LARIB __ ▢▢ __ __ __
   __ __ __ __ __

SECRET NAME:

__ __ __ __ __ __ __ __ __ __ __

 15

SPORTS WORD SPIRAL

A spiral is the best way to throw a football, but it's also a fun way to solve a puzzle. Fill in the answers in the grid on the next page in a clockwise direction (↻). Each word ends at the space where you see the next number. The last letter of one word will be the first letter of the next word. Some answers will have to be written backward or around corners. Answers 1 and 2 have been filled in to show you how it works. When the puzzle is done, you will find a secret nine-letter name written down the shaded middle column of the grid.

1. A sport's best players are chosen to compete in the All-____ Game.
2. The abbreviation for run batted in
3. What a hockey player skates on
4. Philadelphia's National Football League team
5. Neon Deion _____
6. Olympic athletes who finish in second place get a _____ medal.
7. The NBA's super rebounder: Dennis _____
8. These hang from basketball rims.
9. U.S. tennis star Pete _____
10. In most men's professional tennis matches, the winner is the first person to win three ____.
11. A game similar to baseball that uses a 12" or 16" ball
12. A shot in basketball made from directly under the basket
13. The golf score between a birdie and a bogie
14. Colorado's major league baseball team

15. A relief pitcher who finishes up a close win is usually credited with a _____.

16. The man who holds the NFL record for most yards rushing in a season: _____ Dickerson.

17. Soccer's biggest event: the World _____

18. Minnesota Twins slugger Kirby _____

19. Some people play tackle football, others play two-hand _____.

20. Miami's National Basketball Association team

¹S	T	A	²R	B	³I		⁴
⁹						¹⁰	
				¹⁵			
			¹⁹			¹¹	
⁸	¹⁴				¹⁶		⁵
			²⁰				
	¹³	¹⁸		¹⁷			
			¹²				
	⁷			⁶			

SECRET NAME:

___ ___ ___ ___ ___   ___ ___ ___ ___

SKATE SHOT

Chi-Chi Keeta is one *hot* goalie for the Bananas hockey team. He hasn't allowed a goal in four games! Tonight, the Bananas are playing the Gorillas.

Three minutes are left in the game. The Bananas are hanging on to a 1-0 lead. The Gorillas control the puck and are setting up their attack.

Zip! Gorilla center Bob Boone fires a slap shot from the blue line. The puck skips across the ice toward the goal. Chi-Chi is in perfect position to stop it. At the last instant, Pete Pansy, a Gorilla winger, skates in front of the net. The puck hits one of Pete's skates and shoots past Chi-Chi into the right corner of the net. *It's a goal!* Or is it? You're the official. What's your call?

RECORD RACE

Several sports records are as well-known as the athletes who set them. Can you match the athlete (on the left side of the page) with the famous number he is associated with (in the center of the page) and the category in which he set the record (on the right side of the page)? Write the letters of the answers next to the athlete's name. The first one is done for you. (HINT: The sports symbol next to each number is a clue.)

1. Hank Aaron H M

2. Wilt Chamberlain _____

3. Nolan Ryan _____

4. John Riggins _____

5. Rickey Henderson _____

6. Scott Skiles _____

7. Eric Dickerson _____

8. Wayne Gretzky _____

9. Cy Young _____

10. Hack Wilson _____

A. 511

B. 92

C. 30

D. 190

E. 24

F. 2,105

G. 130

H. 755

I. 383

J. 100

K. touchdowns in a season

L. strikeouts in a season

M. home runs in a career

N. yards in a season

O. goals in a season

P. RBI's in a season

Q. stolen bases in a season

R. points in a game

S. assists in a game

T. wins in a career

TO "B" OR NOT TO "B"

There are 15 teams in the NBA, NFL, NHL, and Major League Baseball whose nicknames begin with the letter "B." Can you figure out which teams go in which spaces in the grid on the next page? Use the number of letters in each name and where those letters fit as clues. (We've filled in two teams to get you started.)

When you're done, write the shaded letters in the spaces at the bottom of this page. Unscramble those letters to find the name of a famous tennis player who hits shots like BB's.

5 LETTERS
BEARS
BILLS
BLUES
BUCKS
BULLS

6 LETTERS
BRAVES
BROWNS
BRUINS

7 LETTERS
BENGALS
BREWERS
BRONCOS
BULLETS

8 LETTERS
BLUE JAYS

10 LETTERS
BUCCANEERS
BLACKHAWKS

SCRAMBLED:

__ __ __ __ __ __ __ __ __

UNSCRAMBLED:

__ __ __ __ __

__ __ __ __ __

SPEEDING BULLET

Rochelle "Bullet" Brown is the fastest girl on the Red Rocket Junior High School track team.

Rochelle's team is competing in a meet against the team from Trebble Junior High School. Rochelle has already won the 100-meter race, and Red Rocket leads the meet by one point.

While Rochelle is relaxing after her race, her coach asks her to start warming up again. One of Rochelle's teammates is sick, and Red Rocket needs her to run one more event — the 100-meter hurdles. Rochelle agrees to tackle the event, even though she has never run the hurdles before.

Rochelle blasts out of the blocks at the sound of the starter's pistol. She clears the first hurdle easily but hits the next eight in a row. Rochelle is so mad that she knocks down the tenth, and final, hurdle on purpose.

Rochelle finishes third and scores one point for Red Rocket Junior High. Or does she? You are the meet judge. Does Rochelle's finish count, or is she disqualified for knocking down nine hurdles?

NUMBER CRUNCH

Joe Namath, Bob Griese, Roger Staubach, Terry Bradshaw, and Ken Stabler were five of the greatest quarterbacks in NFL history. They combined to lead their teams to 13 Super Bowl appearances, but they had something else in common: They wore the same jersey number!

The box on this page contains the names and jersey numbers of nine of the best players in football history. Below that is a math puzzle that uses names instead of numbers. Just write each player's number next to his name in the puzzle, then add (+) or subtract (–) as shown. The number you get at the end should be the number worn by the five great quarterbacks.

RB	Jim Thorpe	#1		QB	Fran Tarkenton	10
QB	Len Dawson	16		WR	Charlie Joiner	18
RB	Earl Campbell	34		RB	Gale Sayers	40
LB	Dick Butkus	51		RB	Red Grange	77
TE	Mike Ditka	89				

Mike Ditka (____) – Fran Tarkenton (____) – Red Grange (____) + Earl Campbell (____) – Charlie Joiner (____) + Dick Butkus (____) – Gale Sayers (____) – Len Dawson (____) – Jim Thorpe (____) =

SECRET JERSEY NUMBER _____

23

CHAMPIONSHIP CHALLENGE

The sports figures listed here have all won awards or championships in their sports. Can you find the last name of each star in the word-grid on the following page? The names are written across and up and down. Once you've found them, draw a line through each of the circled names. The lines should spell out the initials of the university that has won more NCAA Division I men's basketball championships (10) than any other school.

Tom SEAVER (baseball)

Byron NELSON (golf)

Sandy KOUFAX (baseball)

Sonny LISTON (boxing)

Johnny MILLER (golf)

Gale SAYERS (football)

Lawrence TAYLOR (football)

Mary Lou RETTON (gymnastics)

Honus WAGNER (baseball)

Bobby KNIGHT (basketball)

Herschel WALKER (football)

Olga KORBUT (gymnastics)

SCHOOL OF CHAMPIONS: ____ ____ ____ ____

```
G D I R V L A E B R H A M D I
O S L G E O M T K O U F A X S
R A W K A H I Y O I F O T E T
Z Y N A S X L W R S A L H U O
A E M L O S L E B E H T K R E
M R I N A Y E T U H B E D S I
Y S E A V E R E T A Y L O R A
V U L I G D N I B H L I C L T
F H M O K R C E M U O F N E Y
B L G B O Z A R W A G N E R A
R I A I V E O K A Y I J U E Z
I S B S A C S I L S T P E T L
E T G R N D M E K N I G H T V
R O M O N R E T E L C E A O E
E N E L S O N S R O T S B N A
D L I H T S F A E J U H R O R
```

YOUR BASE OR MINE?

It's a Little League game between the Blue Sox and the Redbirds. Willie Carson leads off the third inning for the Blue Sox by hitting a line drive single to leftfield. Ronnie Rapp, the next batter, hits a towering fly over the rightfielder's head. Ronnie is a very fast runner. He flies around the bases and easily stretches his hit into a triple.

The problem is that Willie isn't very fast. He has only gone from first to third base. In fact, Willie is standing on third when Ronnie arrives. Seconds later, the Redbirds' shortstop also arrives at third, with the ball. He tags both runners, even though they are both on the bag. You are the umpire. Who is safe and who is out?

RHYME TIME

You may not be able to rap, but you can rhyme. All the missing words in this story rhyme with the word **WALL.** Fill in the blanks to complete the story.

Skye Jones was the best basketball player on the St. Louis Slammers. He stood six feet _____. When the Slammers trailed the Duluth Dunkers by one point with eight seconds left, they knew it was time to give their star player the _____.

Skye saw the seconds ticking away and realized this was no time to _____. He hurriedly faked left, moved right, jumped, and shot. As he did, the man guarding him knocked him down. Skye heard the whistle as he began to _____.

The crowd grew silent, waiting for the official to make his _____. "Foul on the Dunkers!" said the referee. With no time left on the clock, Skye would get two foul shots. He made the first, and swished the second. The Slammers won by one point!

The reporters all crowded around Skye afterward, but he told them to interview his teammates. "We're _____ part of a team," he said. Then his teammates went on to a victory party. And Skye Jones? He just went shopping at the _____.

MYSTERY LINEUP

Picture this! Seven athletes from seven different sports posed together for a picture. The picture below shows the seven athletes, but it doesn't show who plays what sport. Can you use the six clues on the following page to figure out which athlete is which? (HINT: If the clue says a player was sitting to the left of another player, that means your left, not the player's left.)

THE ATHLETES

GOLFER   BASKETBALL PLAYER

HOCKEY PLAYER   BASEBALL PLAYER,

FOOTBALL PLAYER   TENNIS PLAYER

SOCCER PLAYER

THE CLUES

1. The football player and baseball player sat next to each other.

2. The hockey player was sitting just to the left of the soccer player.

3. There were five people sitting between the tennis player and the soccer player.

4. The basketball player sat just to the right of the football player.

5. There was one person in between the golfer and the soccer player.

6. The basketball player was sitting in the middle of the picture.

_____   _____   _____

_____   _____   _____

FLY BALL

Dick and Lisa Penner are playing doubles in the Father-Daughter Tennis Classic. They have reached the championship round and are ready to receive the first serve of the match. Lisa is near the service line, and her father is at the baseline.

The serve sails over the net, and Mr. Penner returns it easily. The teams rally, and Lisa slices a fine backhand shot down the line. The shot catches the other team off guard. The father takes a wild swing and hits the ball, but he hits it much too hard. The ball soars over the net toward Mr. Penner, who is standing behind the baseline.

The ball is obviously going to land out of bounds, so Mr. Penner, assuming that he and Lisa have won the point, catches it with his free hand. You're the referee. Did Lisa and her dad win the point?

SCORECARD SHUFFLE

Joe B. Fan was enjoying his trip to baseball's annual All-Star Game, when suddenly a foul ball came looping toward him and conked him on the head. He was okay, but for a few seconds afterward he saw stars. Then, when he peered down at his scorecard, the names of the All-Stars looked all mixed up. The first names of some players seemed to be next to the last names of others. Can you help Joe by putting the first and last names of these All-Stars in their proper place?

MIXED-UP ALL-STARS:

FRANK PIAZZA   KIRBY BERE

DAVID ALOMAR   TONY THOMAS

JASON CANSECO   WILL WILLIAMS

BARRY PUCKETT   MIKE CLARK

GREG GWYNN   JOSE BONDS

MATT CONE   ROBERTO MADDUX

ANSWERS:

_____   _____

_____   _____

_____   _____

_____   _____

_____   _____

_____   _____

TRIPLE PLAY

Having sure hands in moving letters around will help you solve this three-part puzzle. First, fill in the answers to the clues. Then look at the number under each space. Transfer the letter in that space to the same-numbered space on the following page. When you've transfered all the letters, you should be able to read the trivia stumper. Earn extra credit if you can answer the stumper in the space below it.

1. Another name for a hitter

$\overline{}_{37}$ $\overline{}_{10}$ $\overline{}_{5}$ $\overline{}_{24}$ $\overline{}_{20}$ $\overline{}_{13}$

2. _____ Pippen

$\overline{}_{41}$ $\overline{}_{25}$ $\overline{}_{33}$ $\overline{}_{18}$ $\overline{}_{16}$ $\overline{}_{15}$ $\overline{}_{4}$

3. Win, place, or _____

$\overline{}_{23}$ $\overline{}_{6}$ $\overline{}_{22}$ $\overline{}_{14}$

4. Abbreviation for home run

$\overline{}_{19}$ $\overline{}_{30}$

5. _____ Dykstra

$\overline{}_{9}$ $\overline{}_{29}$ $\overline{}_{1}$ $\overline{}_{36}$ $\overline{}_{11}$

6. A field event: the _____ throw

$\overline{}_{17}$ $\overline{}_{2}$ $\overline{}_{21}$ $\overline{}_{3}$ $\overline{}_{40}$ $\overline{}_{27}$

7. "Oh say can you _____"

$\overline{}_{39}$ $\overline{}_{28}$ $\overline{}_{7}$

8. The New York Yankees' division: the American League

_____

                                   ___   ___   ___   ___
                                     35   38   31   32

9. Another word for jump   ___   ___   ___   ___
                                     34   12   26   8

TRIVIA STUMPER:

___ ___ ___ ___   ___ ___ ___
1   2   3   4   5   6   7

___ ___ ___ ___ ___ ___
8   9   10   11   12   13

___ ___ ___ ___
14   15   16   17

___ ___ ___   ___ ___ ___ ___
18   19   20   21   22   23   24

___ ___ ___ ___ ___ ___
25   26   27   28   29   30

___ ___ ___ ___ ___ ___
31   32   33   34   35   36

___ ___ ___ ___ ___ .
37   38   39   40   41

ANSWER: _____

OUT OF BOUNDS

It's midway through the second quarter of a 1989 NFL game between the Miami Dolphins and the New York Jets. The Dolphins are leading 13-10, and Miami has the ball on its own 35-yard line. On fourth down, the following play takes place:

Reggie Roby drops back to punt. He is standing on the Dolphins' 20-yard line. The center snaps the ball, but he snaps it too high. Reggie tries to catch the ball, but it sails over his head. The ball rolls all the way to the end zone.

Reggie turns and chases the ball. He knows that if a Jet player falls on the ball in the end zone, it will count as a Jet touchdown. When Reggie reaches the ball, he bats it out of the end zone and out of bounds.

You are the referee. What's your call?

NEW JERSEY?

Joey always bought the same sports jerseys as his older brother Jeff. He would be sure to check Jeff's closet before making his next purchase. Find Jeff's newest jersey by picking out the one team name that appears only once on this page.

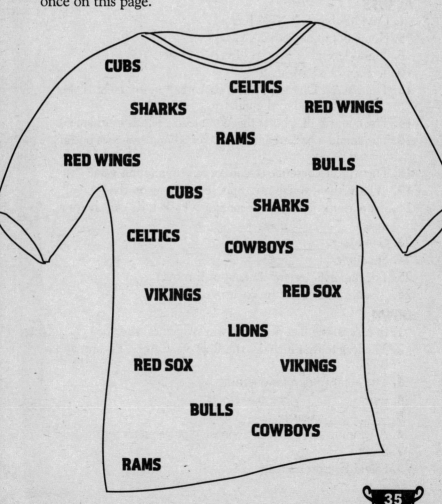

CUBS

CELTICS

SHARKS

RED WINGS

RAMS

RED WINGS

BULLS

CUBS

SHARKS

CELTICS

COWBOYS

VIKINGS

RED SOX

LIONS

RED SOX

VIKINGS

BULLS

COWBOYS

RAMS

CROSSCOURT CROSSWORD

You'll want a courtside seat for this crossword. All of the answers are names or terms used in tennis or basketball. Use the following clues to fill in the puzzle-grid on the next page. The first one is done for you.

ACROSS

1. David Robinson's NBA home
5. Home of pro basketball's Hawks
8. Tennis legend _____ Evert
10. To bounce a basketball
13. The NCAA Division I men's basketball tournament is also called "The road to the Final _____."
14. The country that hosts the Wimbledon tennis tournament
15. The sound a basketball shot makes when it touches nothing but net
18. The word to describe a score of zero in a tennis game
19. In basketball, you're not supposed to hang on the _____.
21. If a player is fouled while making a basket, he can try for a three-_____ play.
23. Game, set, _____
24. Shaquille _____
25. The abbreviation for timeout or turnover
26. A serve that doesn't make it over the net

DOWN

1. In tennis, the first person to win six games wins the _____.
2. The league that includes the Rockets, Celtics, Pistons, and Bulls
3. The abbreviation for overtime
4. One-_____-one basketball
5. _____ Agassi
6. A winning serve that the opposing player can't return
7. Steffi _____
9. David Robinson's team

36

11. Tennis legend _____ Jean King

12. A foul shot is taken from the free-throw _____.

15. U.S. tennis star Pete _____

16. The pro basketball team in Miami

17. A person who wins the U.S. Open, French Open, Australian Open, and Wimbledon has won the Grand _____ of tennis.

20. Kareem Abdul-Jabbar was famous for his sky-hook _____.

22. The name of New Jersey's pro basketball team

37

POURING ON THE JUICE

Suzy Thomas plays forward for the Oranges, a soccer team. In a game against the Hammerheads, Suzy is dribbling the ball down the field.

Stefanie Brody of the Hammerheads runs across the field to block Suzy's path. She gets in front of Suzy near the right sideline.

Suzy is trapped. She can't go straight ahead because Stefanie is right in front of her. She can't dribble to the right because she'll run out of bounds. She can't go left because Stefanie and another Hammerhead player will block her.

Suddenly, Suzy tries a trick. She fakes toward the sideline to draw Stefanie closer. Then she taps the ball to the left, between Stefanie and the other Hammerhead. As the ball goes left, Suzy goes right! She cuts out of bounds and circles past Stefanie. She runs back inbounds and catches up with the ball.

Suzy charges toward the goal, puts a slick move on the goalie, and kicks the ball into the net. You're the referee. Stefanie complains that Suzy broke the rules by stepping out of bounds. What's your call?

MATH MADNESS

In 1984, Miami Dolphin quarterback Dan Marino set the National Football League record for touchdown passes thrown in a season. To find out how many TD passes he threw, complete this puzzle. Read the clues and put the correct number in the space next to each one. Then add or subtract the numbers, as the puzzle tells you to do. At the end, you'll have Dan Marino's magic number.

Number of pins on a bowling alley   _____

Number of players on a baseball team   +_____

Number of points earned for a safety in football –_____

Number of starters on a basketball team   +_____

A perfect score in figure skating   +_____

Number of runs scored on a grand-slam homer –_____

Number of players on each side in a football game +_____

Number of outs in a half-inning of baseball   –_____

Number of points for a touchdown and PAT   –_____

Number of seconds on an NBA shot clock   +_____

Number of Super Bowl winners each season   –_____

THE MAGIC NUMBER IS: _____

FOOTBALL LETTER DROP

This is a football puzzle, so don't drop the ball, just the letters! Below are 12 terms often used during football games. Can you put them in their proper places in the word-grid on the next page? You are given the number of letters in the word or words in parentheses in the list below. After you write each term in its space in the puzzle, one letter from that word or words should be "dropped" into the shaded space directly below it. That letter will appear in the next word or words.

Let's start with QUARTERBACK. Under QUAR-TERBACK are spaces for a six-letter word. But one of the spaces is shaded. That means the letter in that shaded space is the same as the letter directly above it — in this case, it's a "B." Find the only six-letter football term with a "B" as the fourth letter, and go on from there. When you're done, write the letters from the shaded boxes in order in the spaces at the bottom of the next page to spell out the name of a football team.

FOOTBALL TERMS:

HAND OFF (7)   PLACEKICKER (11)

HOLDING (7)   FULLBACK (8)

FUMBLE (6)   CORNERBACK (10)

CLIPPING (8)   LINEBACKER (10)

LATERAL (7)   DEFENSIVE LINE (13)

OFFSIDES (8)   SAFETY (6)

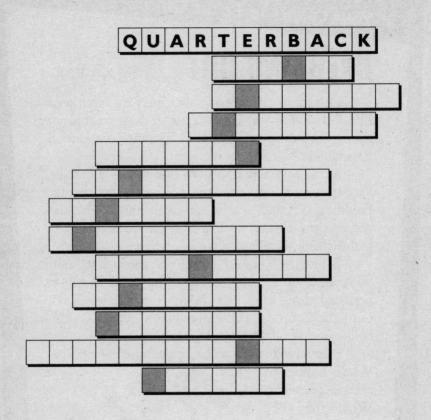

FOOTBALL TEAM:

___ ___ ___ ___ ___ ___ ___

___ ___ ___ ___ ___

OVER AND OUT

Creighton University was playing Southern Illinois University at Carbondale in the semifinals of the 1991 Missouri Valley Conference basketball tournament.

In the first half, Southern Illinois guard Freddie McSwain took off with the ball on a fast break. Freddie is 6' 5" tall, and he can really jump. When he reached the basket, he leaped up and slammed the ball through the rim. *Dunk!*

Before the ball went all the way through the net, however, it hit Freddie on top of his head. *Boink!* It bounced straight up, out though the rim, and back onto the court. A Creighton player recovered the ball and took off on a fast break.

Everyone in the gym looked at you, the referee. What happened? Was Freddie's basket good? What's the call?

SCRAMBLED SUPERSTARS

What's in a name? Sometimes, a weird couple of words. On the right side of this page are the names of 15 famous baseball, basketball, and football players. On the left side are 15 funny word pairs. Can you unscramble the word pairs to find each athlete's *last* name? Print the letter of the correct name in the spaces next to each word pair.

1. LOUD TAN _____		**A.** Paul MOLITOR
2. TREE VET _____		**B.** Herschel WALKER
3. NUT RAVE _____		**C.** Jamal MASHBURN
4. LION LAB _____		**D.** Darren DAULTON
5. BARN MUSH _____		**E.** Frank THOMAS
6. RED LIFE _____		**F.** Boomer ESIASON
7. DRY TASK _____		**G.** Bobby BONILLA
8. NO MEAL _____		**H.** Joe DUMARS
9. RAW ELK _____		**I.** Cecil FIELDER
10. SO MATH _____		**J.** Robin VENTURA
11. RAM SUD _____		**K.** Kirby PUCKETT
12. ROOM LIT _____		**L.** John OLERUD
13. AS NOISE _____		**M.** Jim EVERETT
14. PET TUCK _____		**N.** Karl MALONE
15. DO RULE _____		**O.** Lenny DYKSTRA

SECRET SPORTS CODE

Be a sports detective! Decode the secret clue and find the answer by using the pictures of sports equipment instead of letters. Each piece of equipment — such as a ball, bat, or bowling pin — stands for a letter of the alphabet. Use the decoder key to crack the code and spell out the clue and the answer on the opposite page.

DECODER KEY

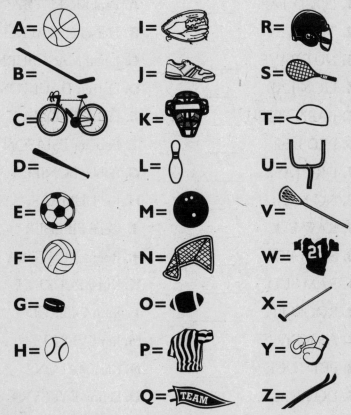

A=
B=
C=
D=
E=
F=
G=
H=

I=
J=
K=
L=
M=
N=
O=
P=
Q=

R=
S=
T=
U=
V=
W=
X=
Y=
Z=

6-WORD CLUE:

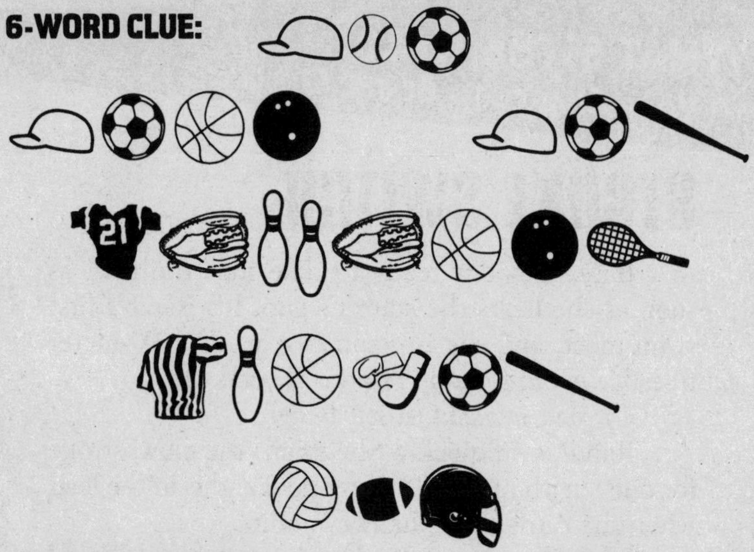

3-WORD ANSWER:

CLUE:

___ ___ ___   ___ ___ ___

___ ___ ___

___ ___ ___ ___ ___ ___ ___

___ ___ ___ ___ ___ ___ ___

ANSWER:

___ ___ ___ ___ ___ ___

___ ___ ___ ___ ___ ___

STROKE SWITCH

Randi Float is ready to dive into the pool as soon as she hears the starter's gun. It's Randi's first swim meet, and she is competing in the 100-meter freestyle event for kids 11 and 12 years old.

On your marks! Get set! Bang!

Randi is off quickly. She swims the crawl stroke for one length of the 50-meter pool and is in the lead when she turns at the halfway point.

With 25 meters to go, Randi is out of breath and her arms hurt because she's been swimming so fast. She doesn't want to quit, though, so she switches to the breaststroke, takes a few gulps of air, and then starts swimming the crawl again.

Although doing the breaststroke slowed her down, Randi still touches the wall in third place, which is good enough to earn her a ribbon. However, a swimmer from another team says Randi should be disqualified because she switched strokes. You're the meet judge. What's the call?

NICKNAME GAME

Of the 16 words listed below, 10 can be placed in the proper spaces on this page to form the nickname of a team in professional baseball, football, basketball, or hockey. Can you pick out the words that can be used to form the nicknames? Write the letters of each word in the spaces where they belong.

EEL	RATE	REAL	CAR
GET	CANE	TAN	RUIN
ONE	KING	HILL	EGG
MOLE	RIOT	ANT	GAL

I. P I ___ ___ ___ ___ S

2. B U C ___ ___ ___ ___ E R S

3. S T ___ ___ ___ E R S

4. B ___ ___ ___ ___ S

5. V I ___ ___ ___ ___ S

6. P A T ___ ___ ___ ___ S

7. G I ___ ___ ___ S

8. P ___ ___ ___ ___ I E S

9. B E N ___ ___ ___ S

10. N U G ___ ___ ___ S

47

FIRST NAME LAST

All the athletes listed on this page have one thing in common — their last names are also popular first names. (The symbol by each athlete's name is the sport he plays.) Can you find the athletes' last names in the word-grid on the following page? The names can be found going forward, backward, up, and down.

Once you've circled all the names, there should be 32 letters left over. Write those letters in order (left to right, top to bottom) in the spaces at the bottom of the next page to find a secret phrase. That phrase contains the names of two more famous athletes with "first name" last names.

Jeff GEORGE ●

Eddie MURRAY ⊘

Vernon MAXWELL ●

Ron FRANCIS ●

Will CLARK ⊘

Byron SCOTT ●

Greg NORMAN ●

Mike STANLEY ⊘

Frank THOMAS ⊘

Sean ELLIOTT ●

Raymond FLOYD ●

LaPhonso ELLIS ●

Scott MITCHELL ●

Chad CURTIS ⊘

Jim KELLY ●

Greg ANTHONY ●

C	N	H	Y	E	L	N	A	T	S
L	A	A	N	T	H	O	N	Y	O
A	M	M	G	E	O	R	G	E	E
R	R	S	R	U	N	K	I	N	L
K	O	I	C	U	R	T	I	S	L
G	N	C	Y	A	R	R	U	M	E
S	E	N	H	A	N	K	F	T	H
S	L	A	A	K	A	T	L	T	C
A	L	R	R	E	O	T	O	O	T
M	I	F	N	L	A	O	Y	I	I
O	S	N	D	L	B	C	D	L	M
H	A	B	E	Y	R	S	U	L	T
T	M	A	X	W	E	L	L	E	H

SECRET PHRASE:

___ ___ ___ ___   ___ ___ ___

___ ___ ___ ___ ___   ___ ___ ___ ___

___ ___ ___ ___ ___ ___   ___ ___ ___

___ ___ ___ ___   ___ ___ ___ ___

49

PENALTY POINT

The Diggers are playing the Golds in a Bantam hockey game. For the past three minutes, the Diggers have been playing shorthanded because center Danny Samuelson was given a five-minute major penalty for cross-checking.

The Diggers penalty-killing unit is tired. The unit has kept the Golds from scoring, but it hasn't been easy. The Golds have some great shooters.

Forward Kigi Yata of the Golds finally gets the puck. He passes to a teammate, who passes it back. Kigi fakes a move to his left, then slips a quick wrist shot past the Digger goalie and into the net. Goal!

Danny pounds his fist in frustration. He starts to leave the penalty box. Players who have been penalized are usually allowed back in the game after the other team scores.

You're the official, and you do not allow him to return to the ice. Why?

FAMOUS FILL-IN

The story on this page is missing some important words. Each missing word is also the last name of a well-known athlete. Look at the list of athletes. Then place their last names where you think they belong.

Barry BONDS
James WORTHY
David CONE
Joe MONTANA

Jerry RICE
Brett BUTLER
Chuck PERSON
Warren MOON
David JUSTICE

Ron DARLING
Steve YOUNG
Mark PRICE
Jay BELL

Rich Mann was perhaps the wealthiest _____ in the state of _____. He was a _____ man (only 21 years old), but he already had his own chauffeur and his own _____. He also had lots of money invested in stocks and _____. What he didn't have, however, was true love. He was in love with a woman, but she believed all he loved was his money.

Then one day, the door_____ rang and there she was. She told Rich that if he could prove that he was _____ of her love, she would marry him. So he walked with her under the light of the _____, bought her an ice cream _____, and showed her that she was more important to him than all the money in the world. "I love you, _____," he said. Soon, they were married by a _____ of the peace, and the crowd threw _____ on the new bride and groom.

The moral of the story is you can't put a _____ tag on love.

USE YOUR HEAD

The Hairpins have an 11-8 lead over the Hornets in a junior high school volleyball game.

A Hairpin player serves the ball over the net. The Hornets hit the ball twice, then slam it back over the net to the Hairpins.

Hilary Hunt of the Hairpins reaches out and hits the ball just before it touches the ground. The ball rebounds off Hilary's arms at a strange angle and hits Hilary's teammate Hedda Hopper in the back of the head. The ball then bounces to another Hairpin player, Helga Hirsch. Helga bumps the ball into the air and Helen Hart spikes it for the Hairpins.

Whew!

You are the referee. Do you allow the game to continue or do you stop the match and call the Hairpins for a violation?

⭐ MVP ANSWERS

PAGES 4-5, SHAQ PACK

(Note: DiMaggio and Wilander can be switched and the solution would still be correct.)

Shaq's school: Louisiana State

```
M A R I N O
O
N
T
A
N
A           D       W     S T A R R     C A R E W
A L O M A R D       I     A       E     A       I
    I     I M       L     N       U     M       L
    C     A V I L A N D E R       S     P D A V I S
    H     G         D     D       C     B       I
    A     G         E     B       H     E       A
    R     I         R     E       E     L       M
S A V A R D         O     R       G     L E W I S
                                  E L           H
                                                E
```

PAGE 6, WHAT'S THE CALL? OUCH!

Strike three, Steve is out! It is ruled a strikeout if a batter swings and misses a third-strike pitch, even if the ball hits him.

PAGE 7, WHAT'S IN A NAME?

1. hit, 2. bat, 3. ice, 4. par, 5. rank, 6. mitt, 7. puck, 8. race, 9. walk, 10. net

PAGES 8-9, OH SAY, CAN YOU "C"?

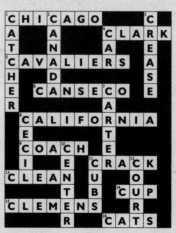

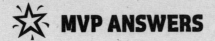 **MVP ANSWERS**

PAGE 10, WHAT'S THE CALL? PASSING FANCY

Gabby's pass was legal and the touchdown counts. A pass can be thrown underhand or overhand, as long as the passer has not crossed the line of scrimmage.

PAGE 11, STATES, MAN!

1. Texas (T, A), 2. Arizona (A), 3. Missouri (M),
4. Kentucky (N), 5. New York (N, O)
Scrambled: TAMNNAO   Unscrambled: Montana

PAGES 12-13, INITIALS SEARCH

1. BB, 2. TD, 3. SB,
4. WR, 5. TKO,
6. AB, 7. FG, 8. PPG,
9. QB, 10. SF,
11. PAT, 12. NHL,
13. HR, 14. RBI,
15. NFL, 16. TO,
17. PO

```
T K O P S        P C        L E
Z V R K H P      L D        Q B
L N A D J P V    W R        P O
I   S     G B G  R A        K A
T   F     R T O  V   R B I  H B
N   E     E O    A M Y H T  W F
O   R     K D    Z I L E D  X U
B B       N H G  P Y        L R
U X N P S H I    A H        F A
S J F L Y L      T Q        G V
B C N F L        F L        H R
```

PAGE 14, WHAT'S THE CALL? A REAL FOUL SHOT

No, Slye does not get another shot, because it is against the rules to fake a free-throw attempt. The Bulldogs get the ball out of bounds on the sideline.

PAGE 15, DOUBLE PLAY

1. Warren Moon, 2. Wilt Chamberlain, 3. Chris Evert,
4. Paul Molitor, 5. A.J. Foyt, 6. Bonnie Blair
Secret name: Walter Payton

54

MVP ANSWERS

PAGES 16-17, SPORTS WORD SPIRAL

1. star, 2. RBI, 3. ice, 4. Eagles,
5. Sanders, 6. silver, 7. Rodman,
8. nets, 9. Sampras, 10. sets,
11. softball, 12. layup, 13. par,
14. Rockies, 15. save, 16. Eric,
17. Cup, 18. Puckett, 19. touch,
20. Heat

Secret name: Brett Hull

PAGE 18, WHAT'S THE CALL? SKATE SHOT

The goal counts because Bob's shot accidentally bounced off Pete's skate. If Pete had deliberately kicked the puck, the goal wouldn't have counted.

PAGE 19, RECORD RACE

1. HM, 2. JR, 3. IL, 4. EK, 5. GQ, 6. CS, 7. FN, 8. BO, 9. AT, 10. DP

PAGES 20-21, TO "B" OR NOT TO "B"

Scrambled:
CIORBKSEREB
Unscrambled:
Boris Becker

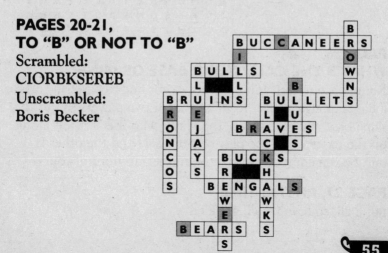

55

 **MVP ANSWERS**

PAGE 22, WHAT'S THE CALL? SPEEDING BULLET
Rochelle's finish counts, and she scores one point for her team for placing third. It is legal to hit the hurdles and knock them down. It is even legal to hit the hurdles on purpose, although that tactic sure slows you down!

PAGE 23, NUMBER CRUNCH
$89 - 10 - 77 + 34 - 18 + 51 - 40 - 16 - 1 = 12$

PAGES 24-25, CHAMPIONSHIP CHALLENGE
School of Champions: UCLA

```
G D I R V L A E B R H A M D I
O S L G E O M T K O U F A X S
R A W K A H I Y O I F O T E T
Z Y N A S X L W R S A L H U O
A E M L O S L E B E H T K R E
M R I N A Y E T U H B E D S I
Y S E A V E R E T A Y L O R A
V U L I G D N I B H L I C L T
F H M O K R C E M U O F N E Y
B L G B O Z A R W A G N E R A
R I A I V E O K A Y I J U E Z
I S B S A C S I L S T P E T L
E T G R N D M E K N I G H T V
R O M O N R E T E L C E A O E
E N E L S O N S R O T S B N A
D L I H T S F A E J U H R O R
```

PAGE 26, WHAT'S THE CALL? YOUR BASE OR MINE?
Ronnie is out and Willie is safe. According to baseball rules, a base belongs to the "lead" runner. If two players run to the same base and are tagged, the player who was farthest along on the bases when the play began is safe and the other is out. So remember to watch the runners in front of you.

PAGE 27, RHYME TIME
tall, ball, stall, fall, call, all, mall

PAGES 28-29, MYSTERY LINEUP

(from left to right): tennis, baseball, football, basketball, golf, hockey, soccer

PAGE 30, WHAT'S THE CALL? FLY BALL

Lisa and her dad did not win the point because the ball was still in play when Mr. Penner caught it. He should have waited until the ball hit the ground out of bounds.

PAGE 31, SCORECARD SHUFFLE

Frank Thomas, Tony Gwynn, Will Clark, Matt Williams, Kirby Puckett, Jason Bere, Greg Maddux, David Cone, Mike Piazza, Barry Bonds, Jose Canseco, Roberto Alomar

PAGES 32-33, TRIPLE PLAY

1. batter, 2. Scottie, 3. show, 4. HR, 5. Lenny, 6. hammer, 7. see, 8. East, 9. leap
Stumper: Name the player with the most career stolen bases.
Answer: Rickey Henderson

PAGE 34, WHAT'S THE CALL? OUT OF BOUNDS

You signal a safety (two points) for the Jets. A defensive team scores a safety when an offensive player loses the ball out of bounds in his end zone (or is tackled in the end zone with the ball).

PAGE 35, NEW JERSEY?

The one team name not repeated is LIONS.

⭐ MVP ANSWERS

PAGES 36-37, CROSSCOURT CROSSWORD

PAGE 38,
WHAT'S THE CALL? POURING ON THE JUICE

Yes, Suzy's goal counts. A soccer player may leave the field and return without penalty as long as the ball does not go out-of-bounds.

PAGE 39, MATH MADNESS

$10 + 9 - 2 + 5 + 6 - 4 + 11 - 3 - 7 + 24 - 1 =$
48 touchdown passes

PAGES 40-41,
FOOTBALL LETTER DROP

Fumble (B), Fullback (U), Offsides (F),
Handoff (F), Placekicker (A),
Holding (L), Cornerback (O),
Linebacker (B),
Clipping (I), Lateral (L),
Defensive Line (L),
Safety (S)
Football Team:
Buffalo Bills

QUARTERBACK
FUMBLE
FULLBACK
OFFSIDES
HANDOFF
PLACEKICKER
HOLDING
CORNERBACK
LINEBACKER
CLIPPING
LATERAL
DEFENSIVELINE
SAFETY

⭐ MVP ANSWERS

PAGE 42, WHAT'S THE CALL? OVER AND OUT
Freddie's basket did not count, and the ball was still in play. Basketball rules say that the ball must go all the way through the net before points are scored.

PAGE 43, SCRAMBLED SUPERSTARS
1. D, 2. M, 3. J, 4. G, 5. C, 6. I, 7. O, 8. N,
9. B, 10. E, 11. H, 12. A, 13. F, 14. K, 15. L

PAGES 44-45, SECRET SPORTS CODE
Clue: The team Ted Williams played for
Answer: Boston Red Sox

PAGE 46, WHAT'S THE CALL? STROKE SWITCH
Randi is not disqualified for switching from the crawl to the breaststroke. Swimmers in the freestyle event are allowed to swim any stroke they choose. Most choose the crawl, the fastest stroke.

PAGE 47, NICKNAME GAME
1. Pirates (rate), 2. Buccaneers (cane), 3. Steelers (eel), 4. Vikings (king), 5. Bruins (ruin), 6. Patriots (riot), 7. Giants (ant), 8. Phillies (hill), 9. Bengals (gal), 10. Nuggets (get)

PAGES 48-49, FIRST NAME LAST
Secret phrase:
Home run kings Hank Aaron and Babe Ruth

```
C N H Y E L N A T S
L A A A N T H O N Y O
A M M M G E O R G E E
R R S R U N K I N L
K O I C U R T I S L
G N C Y A R R U M E
S E N H A N K F T H
S L A A K A T L T C
A I R R E O T O I T
M I F N L A O Y I I
O S N D L B C D L M
H A B E Y R S U L T
T M A X W E L L E H
```

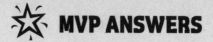

MVP ANSWERS

PAGE 50, WHAT'S THE CALL? PENALTY POINT
Because he received a major penalty, Danny must sit out the full five minutes.

PAGE 51, FAMOUS FILL-IN
Rich Mann was perhaps the wealthiest <u>PERSON</u> in the state of <u>MONTANA</u>. He was a <u>YOUNG</u> man (only 21 years old), but he already had his own chauffeur and his own <u>BUTLER</u>. He also had lots of money invested in stocks and <u>BONDS</u>. What he didn't have, however, was true love. He was in love with a woman, but she believed all he loved was his money.

Then one day, the door<u>BELL</u> rang and there she was. She told Rich that if he could prove that he was <u>WORTHY</u> of her love, she would marry him. So he walked with her under the light of the <u>MOON</u>, bought her an ice cream <u>CONE</u> and showed her that she was more important to him than all the money in the world. "I love you, <u>DARLING</u>," he said. Soon, they were married by a <u>JUSTICE</u> of the peace, and afterwards the crowd threw <u>RICE</u> on the new bride and groom.

The moral of the story is you can't put a <u>PRICE</u> tag on love.

PAGE 52, WHAT'S THE CALL? USE YOUR HEAD
You stop play. In volleyball, a team is allowed to hit the ball three times, but the Hairpins used four hits.